Guided Meditation For Anxiety

Self-Hypnosis and Guided Imagery for Stress Relief, Boost Confidence and Inner Peace and Reduce Depression with Mindfulness and Positive Affirmations

By

Kaizen Mindfulness Meditations

Copyright © 2018
All rights reserved.

No part of this publication may be copied, reproduced in any format, by any means, electronic or otherwise, without prior consent from the copyright owner and publisher of this book.

Kaizen Mindfulness Meditations

Table of Contents

I: Starting Off 4

II: Connect to the Pace of the Earth 10

III: Calm the Chaos 17

IV: Realize Your Path 23

V: Make Space for Health 29

Thank you! 35

I: Starting Off

As you take hold of this moment and begin your journey into meditation, you should feel proud and grateful for you've decided to take your health into your own hands. Congratulations on doing so. By coming to this meditation, in particular, you've decided to work against the intense force of anxiety in your life and you've decided to invite your personal potential to grow, to change for the better. To make the most of this experience, you must start off by calming yourself and collecting your energy. The first step in completing this important task involves assuming the correct position.

If you're able to, come to a comfortable seated position. If you don't have time to sit, first of all, don't worry – this won't take long. In fact, this exercise should feel relaxing and self-assuring rather than contributive to your overall anxiety and it won't take more than 10 minutes away from your focus on other things. If you don't have time to sit, simply stand and feel as relaxed as you can be. Release the weight of your shoulders, let go of any tension in your face, your arms, or your legs, and just allow yourself to feel loose. Allow yourself to feel open and ready to grow and get ready to fully begin.

Close your eyes if you can and if you're completing this exercise on the move, try to look at just one thing in particular as we proceed. In fact, as you can, look out *past* that thing you've chosen to focus on and then let what you're seeing fade from focus completely. You're trying to minimize the distractions around you so you can begin this meditation practice in earnest. Now, turn your attention to your breath, whether you're seated or standing, with eyes closed or open. Turn your attention to your breathing.

How is your respiration flowing now? As you begin to notice it more and more fully, can you tell? Is your breathing even? Is it steady and consistent? Is it deep and fulfilling? Or is it faltering and labored? Do you find yourself breathing without issue or do you accidentally hold your breath a lot? Notice the pace and quality of your breathing and then attempt to make it more consistent.

Consciously, follow each inhalation and exhalation. Imagine that you can see in your mind's eye the air that flows into your body through your nose and mouth, filling your lungs and belly, before exiting out through your mouth or nose once more. "Watch" as this respiration process happens and through the power of your focus, make each inhalation last three seconds and each exhalation last four. Breathe with the aid of this pattern and timing for at least 10 repetitions. If you can sustain this pattern, do so, but you can also simply shift away from that pattern to allow your breathing to assume a pace that's entirely natural to you – as long as it's even and deep and steady.

Once you've increased this conscious and healthy breathing, you'll be faced with the task of centering yourself. As soon as you've established this conscious, fulfilling breath pattern, you'll find it's much easier to determine your more profound and hidden opinions, hopes, thoughts, and feelings, but sometimes these things can distract us from the core of who we really are – the energy that centers us in this lifetime.

Pay attention now to those thoughts and feelings. You've linked with your breath and that breathing focus can always be used to regain traction when your thoughts and feelings become too much, but for now, do try to look directly at the action going on in your mind. What's going on emotionally? Are you feeling relatively neutral or is an emotion taking clear precedence for you? Are you overwhelmed right now or do things feel okay? As someone who suffers through anxiety on a daily basis, you might be coming to this meditation because you just need to prepare yourself for the day. However, you also might be coming to this meditation because you require immediate relief.

For now, just look at what's going on within you. If you're feeling overwhelmed or extremely emotional, breathe deeply for a few inhalations and exhalations. Breathe deeply and let yourself feel calm, confident, and securely safe in this meditative moment. Remind yourself that you really are safe and that the next few moments will help you feel sane, too. Remind yourself that you're working on healing *right now*. As your emotions zip around or stay still and linger around, let their intensity fade. Try to let your deep breathing dissolve any emotional intensities or triggers that may be holding you back from your highest potential. Try to breathe through and *past* these feelings.

Look too at the state of your thoughts. What's on your mind? With the emotion that's most clear to you, what thoughts surround that feeling? What circumstances do you think caused the feeling and thought-pool in the first place? As you can, examine and analyze your thoughts and see what's going on within you. Are your thoughts multiple and constant or are they slow and singular? Is there something particular holding your attention or is there no extra special one thing? As you note what's going on within, gather your knowledge then let it start to fade from attention once more.

In the space behind your conscious thoughts, your goals, and your fears – in the space behind your emotions and behind your eyes where imagination takes place – you find your true center. In this empty, neutral, still, and calm space, you can do and be anything you want to be. Call this your safe space, your happy place, the seat of your soul, or the source of your imagination – this space is where you can take note and begin healing yourself. Through careful attention on the breath and through the silencing of distracting thoughts and feelings, you connect with your center and are left with the singular opportunity of growth, expansion, and transformation.

II: Connect to the Pace of the Earth

With your breathing now constant and steady, with your mind now stilled and at peace, you are ready to connect to the pace of the earth. As someone with high anxiety or troubles interacting earnestly because of incessant concerns, worries, or panic attacks, you likely fight the pace of the earth despite how it constantly makes itself clear around you. Before you can fully heal yourself and fight back against those anxious tendencies, you'll have to reconnect with the pace of the natural and check yourself on what you've been fighting.

Anxious people have the tendency to desire, need, and/or demand control of their lives which causes strife because control is so hard to fully achieve. Anxious people will tend to force themselves to do certain things to decrease worry. They'll establish systems that need to be completed, rules that need to be met, and standards that need to be confirmed before they feel safe to expand or proceed. At the worst of times, anxious people will be *unable* to proceed unless their hopes of control are satisfied. In these ways, anxious people force themselves to work against the pace of the earth, in hopes of saving themselves.

Interestingly, the efforts of anxious people who get to this point go so fiercely against the forces and flows of nature that these individuals lose touch with the most basic principle of healing — the only way *out* is *through*. Anxious people will do well to remember that taking strife out of one's life completely rejects the natural flows of time and space. In fact, these people will come to make great leaps in healing only when they realize that "going with the flow" is about more than just letting things happen. The phrase is more so (and this is especially the case for highly anxious people) about getting in touch with natural patterns, learning to move *through*, and healing through acceptance and personal reprogramming.

When you come to think of your desires now – with your breathing slow and constant, with your distracting emotions and day-to-day thoughts muted – note whether they seem "natural" considering the flows of time and space or if they happen to force things that aren't ready or willing to be. Are these hopes and goals really feasible or do they demand ripping, pulling, or tearing in order to be achieved? What are you really hoping for yourself too if the latter is true?

Sometimes what you consider to be helpful for your anxious nature actually confirms it and makes it all the worse. In some cases like this, the very things you're doing to make yourself "better" are holding you back from any healing. If you do have trouble going with the flow and constantly force yourself through or into situations based on what you think you need, it's time for a reality check. Here, now, as you breathe deeply and consciously, consider how it might be *fueling* your anxiety to keep forcing things to happen in ways that combat what wants to naturally flow around you. Here, now, with patience and love directed both outward and inward, consider how you might be pushing so hard that you're causing yourself stress and pain.

If you think you might truly be working in detriment to natural cycles and hoping for too much, first things first — go through your desires with a reality check. If it seems like your whole world would have to shatter for a certain desire to be achieved, you'll likely be better off rescaling that hope to be more achievable sooner. Additionally, if it seems like you'd have to be a whole new person for a certain desire to be achieved, you could benefit from reexamining whether the hope is actually good for you *now*. Be honest with yourself in this important moment of self-analysis. When you're ready and you're sure that your desires are healthy, achievable, and productive, simply visualize them in your mind.

Go back to that imagination space behind your eyes and visualize your desires as you want them to be, visualize yourself achieving those goals, visualize how you will feel after you've gotten them, and visualize how your life will be changed. Through this imagination-based process, you invite the natural laws of the universe to attract what you want and inherently work in your favor. You choose to radically reject patterns in your behaviors of control-seeking tendencies and you allow yourself to stop fighting against what only wants to see you grow.

As someone who's often anxious, you choose to reexamine your value of waiting. It could be the case that waiting normally causes you extreme discomfort and internal tension. It could be the case that waiting actually makes you have panic attacks when it goes on for too long with no conceivable end in sight. Waiting, however, is a completely natural occurrence that happens for *all* living things. Waiting can be meditative, too. It can give you the opportunity for self-examination, to reality-check, and to ground yourself, but it may still be anxiety-causing for now. Once you re-think waiting in and of itself, you can use it in completely new ways. For instance, rather than forcing your goals to happen through actions that aren't exactly well-timed, you can try actively waiting for the *right* thing to happen. See how waiting benefits you, and let go of your needs to force or control time with each exhalation you release.

For the future, remember to consider the value waiting provides. Try to think of it as providing blank-slate moments to your day when you can inject a little meditation, a little necessary self-healing, a little positive spin. Give yourself permission to hold space for your healing in these moments. Give yourself permission to turn things around for yourself. Don't be too stingy to forgive yourself, too. Anxious people are often *extremely* hard on themselves and it could be their intense desires for control and their high standards for themselves that keep their internal tensions constantly high. It could be, too, that anxious people expect to be able to just *change themselves* for the better.

By expecting to *force* things to *naturally* be expelled from the self, anxious people buy into entirely paradoxical, impossible, or contradictory logic. Instead, you can choose to open yourself to your deeper potential by examining what does and does not work for you as it happens to you. As you come to know yourself better, you'll see those unproductive feelings and urges will fall away naturally and your indifference toward these sensations in the first place will be essential for their dissolution later on. Instead of forcing natural patterns, *expect* them to flow as they will. Instead of forcing yourself, *allow yourself to grow*. Give yourself permission and you'll be surprised by what can happen.

III: Calm the Chaos

As an anxious person, you're particularly attuned to the power of chaos. Chaos is a bitter, omnipresent, and often overpowering adversary in your life, for its presence reminds you how far complete control really is from your experience. Chaos behaves interestingly as a presence or in situations in general. It will always happen, to some extent, but when it does, it draws all attention its way, holds that seat of power, and leaves everyone affected when it leaves.

As an anxious person, chaos is like a vacuum to your energy. Even more so for you than it happens for the average person, chaos zaps your energy and can steal your thunder completely. Chaos simply behaves that way for you and part of the reason for this style of interaction is how *you* respond to the presence of chaos. Of course, chaos is omnipresent – it will not and cannot go away for it's inherent to the nature of the universe. Every experience has its oppositional and balancing experience, so all synchronicity and flow deserve their equivalent balance of chaos. Given that chaos won't be going away anytime soon, it will certainly be you who has to adapt. To make things a little easier, this meditation will present a four-step process to help you do just that.

First, know how chaos makes you feel. Essentially, if chaos were a "trigger" to you, completely altering your day and sucking away your happiness, consider how that triggered response would look. If things got so out of hand you could hardly think, what elements of chaos would have to be present for that situation to exist? Consider the nuances of chaotic situations on your happiness, your flow, your day or even your month, your mood, your patience, your style, and your capacity for kindness. Recognize these pieces of evidence for your relationship with chaos and then we'll use it to your advantage.

Second, invite a space for increased capacity for patience. Based on how you know chaos – or simply losing control – makes you feel, try to imagine what you'd need to be a little more capable around this unstoppable force in the future. Imagine that empty, silent, still space behind your eyes that you established and felt through once more and consider what it would take to maintain that composure, that link to this pure inner space, amongst some of the most chaotic times you've ever gone up against. Invite that space into your life.

Perhaps, for you, this space will be maintained through conscious and meditative patience practices during chaotic moments you come up against. Perhaps, you will establish new and creative defense mechanisms! Perhaps, it will look like carrying a small music player and turning on songs that cue certain emotions whenever you get overwhelmed by chaos otherwise. Perhaps, it will look like stretching for you and you will take a mental step back when you encounter these chaotic moments by extending your neck to feel some relief, relaxing your shoulders, stretching your arms and legs, and more.

Since you are so easily driven to feel anxiety, the stress caused by chaos can bring you intense physical symptoms of discomfort, tension, and panic. This space you plan into your routine to protect yourself will end up providing immediate and needed relief when you go up against all the worst the universe has to offer. Whenever you need to connect to this peaceful inner space, start off by breathing as consciously as possible. Practice active and compassionate patience with the situation and everyone involved, and then breathe your way into your inner sanctuary.

Third, practice an attitude of active acceptance as well as everything else you've been working on in this segment. It may seem like a lot, but it will become almost second nature in no time. As you breathe consciously at this moment and hear these words, you have chosen to be patient and open and receptive. You have already done and learned so much! You have been able to connect with your serene, silent inner space, and you now work on growing your potential, boosting your powers to be able to handle the world a bit differently. In your search for increased potential, you will need to perfect and work with active acceptance on a daily basis.

The more you adopt this attitude of conscious and purposeful acceptance, the more you'll become capable (mentally, emotionally, and personally) at handling anything the universe or others throw your way. In that internal and serene mental space we've been talking about, you hold the potential to shift your overall mentality. Once you're ready to do so, you can adapt constant acceptance as a gesture of healing and patience, and if you need to, *give permission* to yourself to allow this shift. Some overly anxious people are driven to be almost compulsively critical of their surroundings and circumstances, which causes them to force natural laws, timelines, and order, thereby causing themselves undue stress on top of what fate and the universe determine. Through active and conscious permission and acceptance, you'll find the intensity of chaos fading away by the day.

Fourth and finally, visualize yourself literally flying above any chaos if nothing else works. Before you're completely changed in response to chaos, you'll need a way to disarm its intensity on the go. Especially when that chaos happens to be an interpersonal conflict rather than just bad timing or everything going wrong at once, you'll need a foolproof strategy that packs quite the punch. Through an active meditation visualizing yourself with wings or as a bird, you can practice attaining a bird's eye view of any situation. Through this higher perspective, even just lived in the imagination, you'll both emotionally remove yourself from the situation and invite more patient, more understanding logic to assess it when you return. And when you do return, you'll be surprised how small that chaotic moment really was in the grand scheme of things. When you return, you'll be informed and ready for appropriate, forgiving action.

IV: Realize Your Path

Something else that might be causing your constant anxiety could be your progress in life as a whole and how chaos gets incorporated into it. Some overly anxious people are always a bit distracted thinking about all they've accomplished, their current stage in life, and how the two correlate with one another. With all their high expectations and low thresholds for irritation, people who get anxious easily won't respond well to a life that's not going the way they've planned. Of course, this feeling can arise for several reasons, even for the highly anxious person. Life could feel unrewarding, it could feel frustrating or entrapping (as when the individual is stuck in the wrong job), it could feel unfulfilled, with the individual's true potential untapped, and it could feel a variety of other ways all leading up to the individual feeling he or she has failed in some way.

To help correct and heal that feeling, you can try to ascertain *what* in your life is so wrong that you feel so unfulfilled and with that information, you can quiet yourself, discover your true path, and reprogram yourself to align with a healthier, productive, enlightened life with the least amount of anxiety possible. To begin with this mission, make your first step two-fold — re-establish deep quietness and connect to that inner safe space just like you did to disarm chaos in general just a moment ago.

Reconnect with this peaceful inner place by making sure you're breathing evenly, deeply, and steadily. Let any distracting or unrelated thoughts fade from your attention and let any emotions or concerns come and go with the shifting focus of your mind. Switch that focus to your breath and let it only change as your breath does, going inward and blowing outward, in cycles again and again. Through this respiratory focus, you build your inner quiet and make a gateway into your sanctuary.

Along with this quiet, open space comes answers. When these answers to unspoken questions come willingly, as if bubbling up from the emptiness of the universe to greet you, you work against your urge to force and still succeed in your most earnest endeavors to grow. When you receive guidance in this way – from your higher self, spirit guides, God, or otherwise, without force – you will see a path revealed before you that's truer than anything pressured to exist could ever be. You gain the ability to use that guidance to follow your natural path, aligning your life with natural timing without the woes of fear, panic, and force.

As you work to receive these types of answers, something that can help is visualizing a path when you come to your quiet inner space. With eyes closed, go into your imagination – the same inner space that you call your sanctuary, the one that's right behind your eyes – and come to see a path laid out before you. This path could be in the woods, into a city, on a mountaintop, in the desert, at the shoreline of a beach, or anywhere else you desire, but you can't quite see the end of it, that much is certain.

As you look out at the path, you have an innate feeling that will lead you to the answers you seek, even if you didn't voice their respective questions out loud. Still, the universe knows. Your questions are assumed to relate to your potential, your abilities, and your life mission, and when you imagine you set foot on this path in your quiet space, you know you're going the right direction for replies and you feel eager. You sigh with relief and undoubtedly trust that your mind will lead you to the answers you seek.

While you seek to define this calm, quiet inner space and attempt to visualize your path and follow it in your mind, you may struggle and many will do the same. Your inclination for the past long while has been to fight natural cycles of time and force progress when things don't feel quite right. Your urges in this sense have worked against your instincts for patience and slow growth, but you can still get there! Many highly anxious individuals will want to rush this process, but visualization is hard work for even the skilled meditation practitioner. The purpose *is* to have trouble, to work through it, and to get stronger. The *purpose* is to learn and grow with all the ups and downs that entails. As you work through this struggle, be persistent and just don't give up! If you're ready for (and/or *need*) these answers from the universe or from God or your higher self, keep trying at visualizing this path. Keep following it whenever you have a still and silent moment. Keep learning from it whenever you can.

In time, you'll find yourself having an easier time of adapting to chaotic situations. You'll find an increased capacity of being more patient with yourself, with others, with uncontrollable situations, and your progress with life overall. You'll find, too, that letting go of what doesn't serve you becomes simpler, more second nature by the day. Just keep at it! Keep following your path, keep asking important questions (whether aloud or silently), and keep your eyes on the prize

— your own growth and development through these increasingly anxious times. Remember — this too shall pass.

We earlier discussed the importance of practicing active acceptance while resisting the urge to force things along, but something else you can incorporate into your daily practice would be the active practice of letting go as well. Let go of your attachment to distractions whenever they arise and let go of the old ways that used to mean so much to you (but that worked to upkeep your incredible stress on yourself). Let go of what doesn't serve and replace it with new practices (be they meditation-based, respiration-based, mantra-based, action-based, or otherwise), new patience, and most importantly, more spaces to grow, thrive, and blossom.

V: Make Space for Health

As a highly anxious person, you surely know of and trust the connection between body and mind. When you overly stress out about something or let anxiety get the better of you, the body and mind demonstrate to you that they are clearly linked and fueling one another to a terrible extent. Meditation works to both strengthen the connection between body and mind as many says. Yes, this is true, but it is not the only side of the story. Meditation also makes it clear which experiences are which: body-or mind-based or in other words, which experiences come from which realm primarily.

With your practice of meditation, you enable yourself to harness the powers of your mind more easily, with goals intended to enact long-standing healing for your body and soul. Through a five-minute-a-day meditation practice taken over even just a month –without any necessary or substantial mantra, visualization, guidance practice, or otherwise – your body will demonstrate benefits that are clearer to you than sunshine. For now, it will suffice to say that you'll have lowered blood pressure, sustained and healthier heart rate, decrease in headaches or migraines, lessened muscle tension, healthier digestion, less-paralyzing fears, and more restful sleep. And these benefits are just the tip of the iceberg.

Ultimately, it comes down to this — through meditation, you work to heal yourself. While the specific practices of this guided meditation have led you through visualizations and affirmations for success alongside additional, varied techniques, there are still a few more methods that you can put in your meditative toolkit for the future. Along the lines of using visualization to your advantage, you can actually make requests of your healing to the universe through meditation. If you can assess what you want, analyze what it will do for you, and express these things to the universe, you might be amazed at what comes back to you.

Because you know that anxiety has lived, embodied, real-world effects for everyone but especially for you, you likely know what areas of your body are affected the most, too. You surely know where you hold the most tension and how chaos affects you differently based on the circumstances and what you've already gone through that day, week, and year. Focus on these trouble areas (or troubling processing systems) in particular. Diagnose their issues and think of what could be changed to be healthier or more productive. Think, too, of what change would look like and what change is most ideal. Let this specific information inform the healing you seek.

As you learn what in your life needs the most help and you begin to direct your energy toward that healing, you will put part of the responsibility for your growth off onto the universe. By letting go of force and the urge to control, you radically accept that things will happen on their own time, even the healing of your own personality or your overall stress cure.

You *can* relax! You can loosen those joints, release a little tension, and shake off some pressure. You can trust that the universe will begin to respond in line with the requests you've made. The reason why you can believe and trust in this gesture is a little thing called the Universal Law of Attraction. When you meditatively focus, breathe consciously, and call out for things to fill needs in your life, you activate this law which dictates that the universe cannot *help* but respond accordingly when ripples of desire are sent out. Believe in your gifts, send out your wishes, and allow yourself to truly trust in the power of waiting. These are the steps to visualize and actualize your success.

You can attract your own healing and you can connect with something larger than yourself. Through the gift of meditation, you can breathe consciously and direct your power towards anything you desire, be it sanity, stress-relief, serenity, stability, or anything you could imagine.

When it comes down to it, your power is dually held in two closely-related realms — your emotions and your breath. If you believe, trust, and have faith – if you feel openly and peacefully – while you breathe consciously, you can command your world.

Through this practice of unfolded, conscious breathing, you allow yourself to take healing energy into any imaginable area of your life (or others' lives). The limit is only defined by what you can imagine and what you decide is worth your energy. Make sure your limits are as low as possible when you begin meditating by making sure to breathe *into* and *through* any tension whenever it arises. Just like it's problematic to force what you want, it's equally wrong to ignore a truth or opportunity that you know aligns you with your goals. Don't deny yourself just because you're afraid. Go for it because you *know* it is right.

When you experience stress, whether out in the world or within your own body, always remember to breathe into the experience. And then keep breathing until you're through it. It's important to know that when you hold your breath and limit your respiration in moments of high anxiety, you deprive yourself of oxygen, you decrease your potential, and you engage in biologically self-defeating behaviors. From now on, refuse to limit yourself in this way. Accept your potential, draw out and follow your path, and then see what the future has in store. Chaos be damned, for growth is all that matters now and you'll wait as long as you need to for it to become actualized.

Thank you!

Before you go, I just wanted to say thank you for purchasing my book.

You could have picked from dozens of other books on the same topic but you took a chance and chose this one.

So, a HUGE thanks to you for getting this book and for reading all the way to the end.

Now I wanted to ask you for a small favor. **Could you please consider posting a review on the platform? Reviews are one of the easiest ways to support the work of independent authors.**

This feedback will help me continue to write the type of books that will help you get the results you want. So if you enjoyed it, please let me know! (-:

www.ingramcontent.com/pod-product-compliance
Lightning Source LLC
Chambersburg PA
CBHW070041230426
43661CB00005B/711